SERVICE
WHERE IT
COUNTS

Making a Difference
on the Front Line

DAVID E. REED

SERVICE
WHERE IT
COUNTS

Making A Difference on the Front Line

Customer Centered Consulting Group, Inc.
5729 Lebanon Dr., Suite 144 PMB 222
Frisco, Texas 75034

Printed in the United States of America
ISBN: 978-0-9798009-7-9

Credits
Design, art direction,   Melissa Monogue, Back Porch Creative, Plano, TX
  and production   info@BackPorchCreative.com
Copy Editor   Kathleen Green, Positively Proofed, Plano, TX
                                  info@PositivelyProofed.com

Contents

Introduction

"Where the rubber meets the road" or *"The buck stops here"* are phrases that come to mind when I think of front-line employees and customer service. The executives, board members and managers have their role in guiding the organization, but the person answering the phone, a worker checking in patients at a medical clinic, a waitress in a restaurant, or the cashier in a retail store ultimately determine if a customer will come back. The company's reputation in the marketplace is formed by how that customer is treated by the front-line team member day in and day out.

This book is dedicated to all workers who provide services, respond to difficult customers, and deliver on all the plans made in nearly every corporation or nonprofit organization. You make up the largest segment of the work force and may often feel unappreciated or overlooked. Without you, the corporate plans would remain just that, "plans," preventing the delivery of products or services that make up the biggest part of any nation's economy.

The purpose of this book is to give you a true understanding of how personally embracing these service ideas can make your organization successful while also changing the way you view your job, which can help you reach your career goals. Employees who put into practice the following concepts are more likely to move up in the organization and gain recognition as a valued employee or, even better, as a difference maker.

Become a
Difference Maker

Have you ever heard someone say, "I just work here" when they were asked about something or confronted with a customer concern? That phrase should be removed from every employee's vocabulary! If you receive a paycheck from a company or organization, you should have a sense of ownership for the part that you play in that company. You do not have to have stock certificates to demonstrate pride in your position and all that comes with it.

How can you tell if someone understands this concept? You will see behaviors similar to these:

Waitress/Waiter

Whether on a business trip or with my family, we enjoy eating out. Having specialized in the area of customer service, I tend to be very picky about how we are treated at restaurants. Keeping our drink glasses full and bringing our food to our table in a reasonable time frame are the basics. Having knowledge of the menu and being able to offer a suggestion when asked is a plus. I am really pleased when the waiter takes the time to find out what I am really craving and then comes up with a solution that may not be on the menu. For instance, offering to take the fish I was interested in and placing it on a salad instead of a platter with other side items. This was a simple gesture that took a few minutes, but I guarantee they received a nice tip!

Teacher

Being a teacher is one job where the workload is heavy, pay is not the best, and opportunities to change lives occur every day. I had a chemistry teacher in high school named Ms. Sussky. She is one of the reasons I chose to study chemical engineering in college. I still remember one day in class when she was teaching a difficult topic. After looking around and realizing that the majority of the class was not getting it, she closed her book and tried a whole different approach to teaching the concept. The average teacher would have stuck to her lesson plan, regardless of whether the students were learning or not.

Health-care Worker

If you enjoy going to the doctor or having a procedure done at a medical office, you are a very rare person, indeed! For those of you who work in the health-care field, it is easy to forget that your customers are already anxious about being there and could think of 100 places they would rather be than in your office or hospital. It is always refreshing to find a health-care worker who goes out of his or her way to make patients feel comfortable. This can be something as simple as making eye contact with the patient during the check-in process and giving them an accurate estimate of how long they will have to wait to receive treatment.

Call-Center Analyst

When was the last time you called a help desk to say, "Everything is working great today! Thanks for being there for me." It's probably a safe bet that none of you have ever placed a call like that. It takes a special individual to handle working at an inbound call center. The most important characteristic that will distinguish you from others is exceptional listening skills. So many call-center agents simply follow their script instead of truly listening to what the customer is saying. I have been on calls where I needed help with a particular area and the person on the other end of the phone was determined to go through their list of questions, even though they were not relevant to our discussion. It is a pleasant experience when the call-center agent calls me by name and says things to let me know they really heard what I said. You can make someone's day by handling their call in a polite, respectful manner while you resolve the problem that prompted the call.

Field Engineer

You are working in the field to complete a natural gas pipeline connection. You overhear your customer talking on the phone to another vendor and realize that your customer's other project is not going well. The customer hangs up the phone and shares his frustration. You inquire about the other location and get some basic details about the project. You call back to the office and find out if there is another crew available in that general area. After some shifting of assignments, you are able to offer the customer your company's assistance to complete the other project. The customer takes you up on the offer and your company moves into action, thus helping them avoid missing an important deadline. You may have also earned the right to provide additional services for this client.

Retail Store Clerk

A customer is anxious to find an item that is on sale, but that particular item is out of stock. You ask the customer to follow you to the register where you check the stock at several other locations in the area. You find that a store ten miles away has the item and ask the customer if that store is convenient for him to go and make his purchase. He responds that the location is on the way to his next stop, so you immediately pick up the phone to have that store hold the item at the checkout counter. You apologize to the customer for any inconvenience and wish him a good day.

Grocery Store Checkout Clerk

One of the main customer turnoffs in any business is waiting a long time to check out or receive what they are attempting to purchase. I always appreciate it when a checkout clerk at a grocery store notices there is a long line of customers waiting to check out at their register and she immediately calls for a backup checker. She understands that the No. 1 source of customer frustration is waiting in long lines. I also appreciate it when they take the time to look at you and ask you if you were able to find everything, truly interested in your response.

Waste Management Driver

Most people don't think about customer service when talking about garbage pickup, but the truck driver can actually do a lot, both positively and negatively, to affect the customer's perception of the company. When you drive a vehicle for a living, do you sometimes feel that you "own the road" and tend to expect others to move out of your way? Showing some common courtesy by letting someone back out of their driveway before moving past can leave a customer with a positive feeling. In my neighborhood, the trucks have the automated collection arms that pick up the trash can and dump it in the truck without the driver leaving the vehicle. On occasion, we will have more trash than will fit in our one can. It has made my wife's day several times when she has met the truck by our can, and the driver allows her to place additional trash in the can for a second dumping.

Hotel Front-Desk Team Member

Checking into a hotel, whether on a business trip or family vacation, often sets the tone for the entire stay. With my work, I end up staying in a hotel 50+ nights a year and have seen some good and some bad front-desk workers. What makes this experience a positive one? It starts by how they greet me when I approach the counter. A simple statement like, "Welcome to our hotel. How was your trip today?" is a good start. Just recently we had a nice experience that exemplifies how a hotel worker can go the extra mile. On a family vacation, we stopped to spend the night at the halfway point on our way home. We had arrived early enough to see a movie, so we checked with the front desk about the location of a movie theater in town. Not only did she tell us where to go, but she reached in her desk and pulled out a printed set of directions to get us to the theater and then back to the hotel. This may be a frequent question, but someone took the initiative to type up the instructions and have them ready for their guests. A simple act, yes, but it ensured we had a good evening while also increasing the likelihood that we will return to this hotel again.

Child Welfare Worker

During my days in Florida I had the privilege of working for an organization that is responsible for looking out for the most vulnerable members of the community: children. This is a very difficult job, and the employees have to experience some of the worst situations imaginable: the abuse and neglect of kids. Even as difficult as this is, the workers and their organizations can still benefit from practicing great customer service. Their customers may include children, other agencies and foster parents involved in caring for children who were removed from their original homes. Communicating in a timely manner, including returning phone calls and e-mails, is probably one of the most significant things they could do to serve their customers. Even when they do not have all of the answers, a simple call acknowledging the message or request for information will go a long way to having a satisfied customer.

Veterinary Office Receptionist
No matter how minor the reason for bringing our dog, Cocoa, in to the vet, we always receive a call the next day from one of the front-office workers. They are genuinely interested in our dog's health and are calling to make sure everything is okay. Nice touch!

Fast-Food Worker
There are few places where I appreciate good customer service skills more than in a fast-food restaurant. Maybe it's because I generally don't expect exceptional service with my burger or sandwich, so when I do experience a pleasant worker who takes my order and makes eye contact while asking how my day has been, I am truly surprised. If the order is delayed, it also is nice when the order taker says, "Sir, it will be a few minutes. Why don't you fix your drink and have a seat? I will bring the rest of your order to you as soon as it's ready."

Delivery Driver

Driving a vehicle that displays your company's name and logo is both an opportunity and a risk, depending on how you are behind the wheel. Whenever I see a truck cut someone off in traffic, I am sure to notice the company represented by the driver. The opposite is also true. When a delivery driver goes out of his or her way to allow other drivers to change lanes or enter the road, I notice the company and am more likely to give them my business. Driving a car or truck for a living can be a difficult job, but you need to realize that you are a moving billboard for your company, and your actions can encourage or discourage hundreds of people each day to do business with your organization.

MAKE SOMEONE'S DAY

There is hardly a job where you don't have the opportunity to make someone's day nearly every time you report to work. When you are heading to work, what are you thinking?

A. "Another day at work to get my paycheck. Eight hours and then I can head back home and enjoy time with my friends or family."

B. "Another opportunity to go to work and have a positive impact on someone else's life. I wonder who I will come in contact with today?"

I am not suggesting that every day at work is going to be a fun, positive experience, but the attitude that you have as you prepare for your day will determine the type of day you have more often than not. It is a choice!

You have the power to decide if you are going to be an average employee just doing enough to get by or if you go to work each day with a goal to serve your customers and make a difference. Choose to be a Difference Maker!

Serve Your Fellow Team Members

The employees who have learned the secret of serving others will be sought-after team members in almost every company. The gift of service is very rare in today's homes and workplaces. Why is this the case? Because we are all taught from an early age to look out for ourselves. Whether from TV commercials, news clips, sports heroes renegotiating their contract or a learned survival tactic after being stabbed in the back, most employees enter the workplace feeling the need to fight for what is theirs.

You may have had the opportunity to work with someone who chose a different path: Someone who has learned the secret of serving others. But you may think, "If I don't look out for my own interests, I will be stepped on and become a doormat." That may be true in some cases, but the individuals I have encountered who have developed a life of serving others are often very confident and secure in their own abilities. They move up the company ladder, eventually surpassing those who were self-centered and playing company politics. It may take awhile, and it may seem that the bad guy is being rewarded, but it all comes around eventually.

Many of you may be great at serving others in your family, church or volunteer organization, but you may wonder, "How do I serve others in the workplace?"

Let me ask you a few questions.

1. When a new employee starts in your department or on your team, what thought and response best describes how you feel?

    a. I may not admit it, but I feel threatened by the new hire and will let them struggle to pick up the knowledge that I have learned over the years.

    b. I don't have time to get my own work done. He or she will have to get it on their own.

    c. I consider having a new team member an opportunity for all of us to become better. I will go out of my way to make them feel welcomed and comfortable in their new job.

2. You have been working hard on a five-person team to reach a difficult deadline. The team makes the goal, but you hear that one team member has been privately talking to management and taking credit for more than their fair share of the success. How do you respond?

    a. You secretly gossip with the other team members and attempt to discredit this employee.

    b. You let it go and trust that management will see through this and eventually know the truth.

c. You find the time to privately visit with the manager and set him or her straight on who really was behind the team's success.

3. You normally have a very tight schedule and find it difficult to get your assigned work done every day. The manager in your department saw your struggles and shuffled the work assignments to take some tasks off your plate. You now have a comfortable workload. How do you react?

a. You are relieved that the manager finally saw the situation and made the adjustments. You relax and focus on your new tasks.

b. You are grateful for the shift in work, but you realize that other team members are still overworked, so you seek out ways to help them once you finish your work.

You can probably guess how someone who serves others would respond. (Answers: c, b, b.) It is amazing how a workplace can be transformed when just one team member starts to serve his fellow teammates. The job becomes more enjoyable when you are able to relax and focus on how you can contribute to the success of the team, rather than worry each day about how someone may be taking advantage of you or treating you poorly.

The key is to take a long-term view of your work. If you honestly believe that doing a great job and helping others be successful will ultimately be a winning formula, then it will make coming to work a whole lot easier. As the great motivator Zig Ziglar often says:

"You can have everything in life you want if you will just help enough other people get what they want."

When No One
Is Watching

How do you perform when your supervisor is not around? Your answer to this question says a lot about your character and your potential for advancement within the organization. Every employer is looking for team members who take initiative, deliver excellent customer service and represent the organization well. It is a bonus when they find front-line employees who will do all of these even if the supervisor is not observing their performance.

Most employees are going to do a good job when someone is watching, but the best team members are going to do the right thing even when no one is looking over their shoulder.

Most employees are going to do a good job when someone is watching, but the best team members are going to do the right thing even when no one is looking over their shoulder. The funny thing is that even when you don't think that you are being watched, customers and potential customers are almost always observing your behavior and how you treat each other and your customers.

My wife and I just entered that "fun" stage of life when we have a teenager in the house. We are blessed to have our son, Tony, who is very responsible and, generally speaking, makes wise decisions. Each week it seems that our household schedule gets busier. There are sports activities, school functions and new social opportunities that Tony wants to join in with his friends. Tony has learned that if he does the right thing and we hear positive feedback from our friends about how he conducts himself when we are not around, he will gain additional freedoms and responsibilities.

The same thing applies at the workplace. If you are an employee working in a small retail establishment, the owner of the store will be looking for people he or she can really trust. There will come a day when they need someone to open, close or just run the store when he or she can't be there. They will probably start out with short periods of time leaving you in charge. If everything seems to go smoothly, they will extend that time and add more responsibilities to your plate. If they receive some bad reports or find out that things did not go as they would have liked, they will probably not trust you in a position of responsibility again.

While I was in high school, I had the opportunity to start a small company painting houses. I had four or five of my best friends join me, and we would paint 10 or more houses each summer. We would often try to wrap up the painting by noon on Friday and go spend some time skiing at a nearby lake.

I can still remember one week in the middle of the summer. We had worked long hours for two weeks to finish a large job. It was noon on Friday and we had completed the house and had packed up all of our equipment and strapped the ladders on top of my Chevy Chevette. (It was a bit crowded with four big guys and all of our stuff!)

As I would do at the end of every job, I walked around the house with the customer and made sure he or she was happy with our work. This particular week is one I will remember for the rest of my life. Earlier that day, I was on the roof finishing some painting when I noticed that we had not put the final coat on the backside of the wood part of the chimney. It was something that the customer would never have figured out.

I was faced with a decision: I could act as if we were done, collect the check from the customer and head to the lake, or I could tell the team to unpack the equipment, get out the paint, crawl up on the roof and finish the job, clean the brushes, and repack the car, delaying our recreation at the lake.

No one other than myself would have ever known if I had chosen the easy road, but my conscience would not let me do anything less than my best. We unpacked our gear and finished the job. The team moaned and groaned when I broke the news, but later everyone felt good about our decision and we still enjoyed some time together on the lake.

It all boils down to one thing: **Your integrity will be evaluated by what you do when no one else is watching. Choose the correct path! Deep down, you know the right thing to do. Don't compromise your character for a temporary gain.**

Service Where It Counts

Leave It at the Door!

I doubt that any of you reading this book makes it through a month without having a bad day or having difficult things thrown at you in your personal life. If you have a pulse and are living in this fast-paced world, tough times are going to come. Problems can have many sizes and levels of intensity and could include things such as:

+ Financial problems

+ Relationship issues

+ Challenges at a second job

No one wants to hear daily details of your personal life, especially if you are constantly complaining about someone or something. An occasional comment or story is okay. This concept not only applies to those problems in our lives, but is almost as important when it comes to our successes. This does not mean that you can't share any personal stories with your co-workers. The key is to use common sense when thinking about whether to share something at work.

Remember, even if you have several close friends on your team or in your department, there will almost always be someone in your work area who would prefer to not hear about your personal life.

This is even more important when you consider your customers being on the listening end of your complaints or personal stories. Very few customers have an interest in a total stranger's life, regardless of how interesting you may think you are!

This includes conversations between co-workers in the customer's presence. I can remember a situation several years ago that illustrates this point. I was at a department store and was trying to get some help from one of the store employees to pick out a gift for a family member. There were two employees who obviously were good friends that had not seen each other since the previous week. One of the employees was sharing a story about her weekend. I patiently waited while listening to the details about a "hot" date that the one had been on Saturday night. I finally asked for some help and was told, "I'll be with you in a minute." They went on for another 20 to 30 seconds completing their story.

I can appreciate that you spend the majority of your lives at work and may develop some strong personal relationships with your co-workers, but when a customer is present, your attention must be entirely on serving him or her. There usually will be slow moments for you to catch up with your friends at work.

In summary, everyone should try to make it a practice to leave their personal issues and stories at the door, and only share in very selective situations when it is not distracting from meeting your customers' needs.

Service Recovery

Martin Luther King, Jr. once said:

*"The ultimate measure of a man is not where he
stands in moments of comfort and convenience,
but where he stands at times of challenge and controversy."*

When things are operating smoothly, most employees can meet customer expectations. But when there are problems, the true character and quality of an individual and even his or her organization become visible.

There will be errors and problems, but recovering from these situations is what determines if a client will stay with your company or choose the competition.

Who will most likely be the first to hear of a service problem or get wind that a customer is not happy with your product? The front-line employee ... because they interact with customers on a regular basis. This is why great organizations such as the Ritz-

There will be errors and problems, but recovering from these situations is what determines if a client will stay with your company or choose the competition.

Carlton or Disney spend a lot of time and energy ensuring that every employee understands how to first recognize a problem and then knows what to do to "recover," or satisfy the customer's needs.

There are way too many people who – when exposed to a problem with a customer – shrug their shoulders and think that the problem belongs to someone higher up the organizational chart. Even if you don't have the authority to solve a problem, how you handle the encounter with the customer can make or break their perception of your entire organization.

How do you know that a customer is not happy or that there is a problem with your product or service?

+ **Be Observant.** About 85 percent of all communication comes through something other than words. This is also true of your customers. Watch their body language, notice their facial expressions and, easiest of all, listen to them when they share their opinions and feelings. Consider yourself a detective on a mission to find customers who are less than thrilled with your organization. The recovery process can only begin after identifying an upset customer.

+ **Do Something.** The average employee, when confronted with a customer-service problem, will look the other way. The worst thing you can say is, "That's not my job!" Even if the problem did not start in your area, you are the representative of the company or organization. The exceptional employee will kick into high gear to resolve the issue so that the customer is no longer upset. They will become a fan of your company. Great organizations will make it easy for front-line employees to find the resources necessary to resolve customer complaints.

These simple steps should be followed when you are faced with a service problem, regardless of the error's source:

1. **Listen to the customer.**

   A customer who has experienced a problem with your organization needs someone to listen with the goal of understanding. Even if the customer is calm and not upset, listening is the first step toward resolving a problem. (For more help in responding to a customer who is clearly upset with you or the company, see Chapter 9: Handling Difficult Customers.)

   If you think you have already heard that particular customer issue 1,000 times, let the customer explain their situation completely without interruptions. Use your good listening skills to paraphrase back the key points of the message to ensure you really have captured the true problem.

2. **Take notes.**

   When possible, take some notes to make sure you remember the important details. This includes the customer's name, contact information and details about their transaction or experience. The goal is to gather enough information to allow you to follow up within your company without having to go back to the customer for more details. If the problem is out of your area of expertise, you may have to gather their name and number and a summary of the problem and let them know someone will contact them.

3. Involve others.

Once you have the basic information, engage your team to resolve the issue and save the customer. If you are fortunate enough to work in an area that directly deals with the customer's problem, you may be able to resolve the problem and get back to the customer yourself. When communicating with other members of your organization, it is your job to accurately relay the customer's information and feelings. Remember, you now represent that customer. If someone else has to contact the customer, do everything possible to avoid the customer having to re-explain their situation. That can be a source of frustration and leave the customer wondering why they spent the time talking to you in the first place.

4. Own the follow-up with the customer.

When possible, it is great when the initial person who recognized the customer problem and spoke with them can close the loop once a solution has been found. In many cases, this is not possible and you have to hand off responsibility to another team member. However, if this is the case, I would encourage you to at least give your name and contact information to the customer and let them know that they can give you a call to check on the progress if they don't hear from someone within a set amount of time. This makes a connection between you and the customer and prevents them from having to explain their situation to yet another member of your organization.

Those individuals who view customer problems as a challenge to be conquered rather than an annoyance or interruption to their day are the ones who enjoy their jobs and become valuable representatives of any organization.

A Sense of Urgency!

As I write this chapter, I am sitting on an airplane heading out to visit a customer. After parking the car, jumping on the shuttle, checking my bag, and then making it through security, I arrived at my gate with plenty of time to spare. I was able to relax and get some work done for a few minutes before it was time to board the plane.

The gate agent came on the speaker and announced that we were going to be delayed due to a mechanical problem with the plane. We later learned that they were changing a flat tire. Twenty minutes after that announcement, she let us know that they had found another plane, but we were going to have to walk halfway down the terminal to the new gate. I was thrilled that we were only going to be delayed 45 minutes.

Wishful thinking! We arrived at the new gate only to learn that this aircraft was also having a mechanical problem. After another 30-minute delay, we were allowed to board the plane. This is where the problem really started!

We were all seated ready to get on our way when they announced that the luggage had not been transferred from the original plane. I watched out the window as several of the baggage handlers walked around, obviously in no big hurry to put our bags on the plane. They visited and joked around while our bags sat in the luggage carts ready to be loaded. It was another 30 minutes before they loaded the bags. (This was not a big plane.) They had to know that we were running very late when the bags were pulled off another plane, but this did not seem to matter to them. They needed to have a sense of urgency.

Contrast that with another airline that I fly on occasion. ALL of their team members get this concept! When you arrive at a gate on this airline, you can watch their team kick into high gear to get you off the plane. The door is usually opened within 30 seconds of arriving at the gate.

Let me give you another example. Several years ago, I had the privilege of delivering customer service training for a valet parking group that served the headquarters building for one of the nation's largest corporations. Valet parking can be a tricky business when you consider that the No. 1 customer turnoff is a long wait. More often than not, the demands on their services come all at once when an event is getting ready to begin or concludes at the end of the evening.

If you were waiting for your car in a long line of customers and you saw the valet attendants walking slowly or taking a break, how would you feel? If you are like me, you would probably be irritated that things were taking so long. Now, if you saw the same workers hustling back and forth from the parking lot to bring up the customers' cars, sweating and obviously exhausted, how would you feel then? You would be much more understanding of the delay.

Our society has become very impatient! (For example, how many of you have found yourself waiting impatiently for something to finish in the microwave, or worse, you pull the food out before the timer goes off?) We all want things right away and don't like to wait. This applies to checking out at the grocery store or having your call answered at a call center. It is critical that every member of the team understands that delivering your service or product in a safe but quick manner is key to pleasing your customers.

> *It is critical that every member of the team understands that delivering your service or product in a safe but quick manner is key to pleasing your customers.*

Engage the Customer

Several years ago I was asked to help a theme park improve its customer service. To get started on this project, I spent two days in the park as a tourist enjoying the various shows and attractions. One of the things I tracked was the percentage of employees who made contact with me, or "engaged" me, through eye contact or words. What I observed was interesting. It seemed that the employees were more interested in talking amongst themselves than interacting with their guests. Out of a possible 44 employee interactions, only four took the time to say hello or at least nod or smile. The remaining 40 employees were talking to other employees or daydreaming about what they were going to do when they got off work.

Let me give you a few examples of how you can engage your customer.

✦ **Restaurants.** I know that waiting tables in a restaurant is a difficult job and can really wear you out by the end of your shift. One of the keys to becoming a great waitress or waiter is in the way you interact with your customers. This starts with the host or hostess when they greet you at the entrance to the restaurant. Do you take the time to say hello to each guest, regardless of how busy you may be? When you are escorting a family to a table, do you take the time to visit with them as you are walking to the table, or are you so far ahead of them that they may lose sight of you?

When I want a refill of my water or soft drink, I will typically watch for my server as they finish up at a nearby table. I have noticed that the best servers will take a quick look at their assigned tables to see if a customer is trying to get their attention. That makes it easy for me to make eye contact with them to let him or her know that I need something. I realize that this can be a distraction and delay turning in a food order or running a credit card, but the best servers have learned how to multitask and juggle multiple requests without losing track of what they are doing.

✦ **Retail.** During an eight-hour shift in a large home-improvement store, you can interact with hundreds of customers. It may seem that you are constantly bothering your customers by asking them if they need some assistance, but most customers would prefer to be asked multiple times instead of being ignored. One of the clues that every retail worker should learn to pick up on is when you see a customer staring up at the aisle signs trying to locate a particular product. That is an invitation to ask the customer, "May I help you find something?" If possible, it is always preferable to take the customer to the correct aisle instead of simply giving them an aisle number.

Once you finish getting the customer to the correct location, always follow up with, "Is there anything else I can help you with?"

✦ **Grocery Store.** Regardless of your job title, everyone who works in a grocery store is in the customer service business. When I worked at Walt Disney World™, they would train every employee (called "Cast Members") that we were responsible for assisting a guest, even if that was not our primary role. Who do you think knows the Disney parks the best and answers more questions for directions than any other cast member? If you guessed the team members who picked up trash and swept the walkways, you would be correct. These important representatives of the Disney organization need excellent communication skills every bit as much as those working in the official "Guest Relations" office.

The same thing applies at a grocery store. I had a pleasant experience recently when I was out of town and needed to pick up a few items at a local store. A young man was busy stocking the shelves, but he took the time to notice that I was trying to find something and immediately stopped what he was doing and asked, "Sir, can I help you find something?" He left his aisle and took me to the item I was trying to purchase.

Checking out quickly is just as important. When a checkout clerk has an empty lane, it is a great time to engage the customer by waiting in front of the lane and asking, "Are you ready to check out?" If the answer is "yes," they can reply, "I can take care of you" and guide the basket into the lane.

Engaging or Pestering?

When it comes to engaging the customer, one of the most difficult things is knowing when they want help and when they would prefer to be left alone. If you are a waitress or waiter, you must learn to read your customer's body language. If you try to engage in light-hearted conversation and they do not make eye contact but continue to focus on the members of their party, it is a good sign that you should keep the chitchat to a minimum. If they, on the other hand, look at you and respond to your comments or ask a question about your favorite items on the menu, it is safe to assume that they are open to talking with you.

There is always a balance to shoot for when engaging customers, especially if you are working on commission. The goal for commissioned salespeople is to assist the customer on their terms to the point that they do not realize you are working on commission. If their response is, "I am just looking," that is a universal signal that they want to be left alone. An appropriate response would be, "That is fine. I don't want to bother you. If you need something, I will be right over here and would enjoy assisting you. Take your time."

One of the skills that will separate an average customer service employee from the best is learning to be sensitive to a customer's needs. Often this means anticipating their next move or request and being ready to kick into gear to assist them. Remember, you are less likely to upset a customer if you engage them than if you ignore them!

Remember
Your Grandma

We all want to be treated with kindness and respect. So many times we get caught up in job demands and forget this basic principle. We are more concerned about our needs than those of our customer. Earlier this week I was leaving Dallas and flying to Tampa, Florida. It was one of those very early morning flights that I always wonder why I picked such an awful time to fly because I had to wake up and head to the airport so early! On the upside, one advantage is that the check-in lines tend to be shorter. I was doing the self-check-in when I observed behavior that really made me angry.

There was an elderly lady who was by herself and obviously not a frequent flyer. She needed some assistance checking in, but had accidentally gotten into the self-check-in line. She approached the counter to ask for help, and one of the agents very rudely informed her that she needed to go wait in the other line. The agent was doing absolutely nothing and could have helped the lady or walked her to the correct place to receive assistance. Instead, the agent loudly repeated her command that she was in the wrong lane and pointed to the full-service line. There was no one in line, but the agent made her navigate through the roped-off lanes just to be called to a counter that was no more than 15 feet from where she had started! Before making my way through security, I made sure the elderly customer was taken care of.

Whenever I witness something like this, I think, "I wonder how she would like her own parents to be treated if they were flying by themselves?" I think about my own grandma and hope that she has someone with some compassion and kindness ready to help her when she is traveling.

Ask yourself this basic question: "How would I like to be treated if I was in the same situation?" Granted, it can be tough on the front lines handling the customers while also trying to meet the demands of your boss at the same time. This can make even the friendliest person develop a sour attitude on occasion. But don't take it out on your customer! In the vast majority of cases, they have done nothing to deserve an unkind word or action.

If you develop a habit of treating every customer with kindness, you will find that your job is much more enjoyable, and you will receive many more "thank you's" and compliments from satisfied customers than harsh words or complaints from upset customers.

If you honestly look at yourself in the mirror and say, "I want to be nice, but I seem to always fall back into my critical nature and find it easier to complain than to do something positive," then I have a simple trick to help you become a kinder person. For the next 30 days, make it a habit to find two people to help or compliment during your normal daily routine. Write these down in a simple notebook. After 30 days of going out of your way to compliment someone else, you will find your overall attitude shifting from the negative to the positive.

I have to use this strategy myself. The majority of time, I am working with organizations to find things that are broken or need significant improvement. If I don't watch out, I can be very negative and critical, especially when it comes to customer service issues.

For the next 30 days, make it a habit to find two people to help or compliment during your normal daily routine.

I still remember one time I was trying to apply the "Two Compliments a Day" policy when I was traveling. I was in an airport and waiting at a gate that had become very familiar from regular flights to the same location. I had noticed a woman who was always responsible for cleaning this set of gates. She did a great job and went above and beyond to make sure all trash was picked up and even the rim of the trash can was clean. One day I stopped her and just thanked her for making this gate area clean so I could be comfortable working while waiting for the plane. You would have thought I had given her $100! She got a big smile on her face as she moved her cart on to the next trash can.

If you treat people with kindness often enough, it will have an impact on your own attitude and behavior as you interact with your customers and co-workers. Very few people have ever complained about someone being nice!

Handling the Difficult Customer

Unfortunately, not every customer is easy to deal with! I have heard someone say, "My job would be great if I didn't have to deal with those customers!" Customers can become angry for a variety of reasons:

+ **Poor product quality.**

    Sometimes the quality of the products sold by your company does not meet your customer's expectations. You may not have anything to do with the design and manufacturing of your physical products, but every employee is responsible for standing behind what their company sells and working to resolve customer issues.

+ **Service delivery error.**

    I wish we could work for organizations where every team member was at the top of their game each day and never made a mistake. Service delivery errors can happen when any employee develops a bad attitude and loses focus on what they are doing. And, despite having the best intentions, errors also occur when employees simply make a mistake due to a lack of training or human error.

✦ Inaccurate expectations set.

There are times when the sales and marketing divisions within your organization get a little carried away with promises made to the customer. Several years ago when I was living in Florida, we planned a trip to one of the state's many beach resorts. I checked on the Internet and found what appeared to be a great place at a reasonable price. They advertised a "Two Bedroom Suite with a Partial Ocean View."

When we arrived at the hotel, we got our room assignment and eagerly went to check it out. That's when we realized their marketing people had never actually been in our room! The only way I was going to see the ocean was if I leaned over my balcony and strained to see an occasional wave. As for the "Two Bedroom Suite," the only thing that made this have a second room was one of those old portable divider walls that separated the bed from a couch.

Needless to say, we were not happy customers and promptly left the hotel for a better option down the road.

✦ Expectations not met.

Even when we do everything possible to set accurate expectations, there are those times when we fall short. This can happen with a problem on our side or when a customer develops his own wrong expectations. In either case, we have an upset customer that we have to deal with.

✦ Dealt with an uncaring worker.

Those of us who are trying our best to do the right thing and serve our customers would like nothing more than to have everyone else at our company share our passion. Unfortunately, that will never be the case. For a variety of reasons, we will have to work with individuals who have lost their desire to serve the customer and positively represent our organizations. We all have to "clean up" after a co-worker makes a mess of a situation.

✦ They are unhappy about everything in life.

A small percentage of customers will never be happy. No matter what you do and how hard you try to please them, they will not be satisfied. You never know what is going on in someone's life, so I encourage you to do your best, don't take it personally, and cut them as much slack as you can.

Regardless of why customers are unhappy, it's the front-line employee's job to make things right. Can you succeed in every situation? No, but your chances will increase dramatically if you follow these steps to handle the customer:

> *Regardless of why customers are unhappy, it's the front-line employee's job to make things right.*

1. Listen

✧ Listen carefully without interrupting the customer. Interrupting appears defensive and tends to add "fuel to the fire."

✧ Get into listening mode, stop what you are doing and give your full attention. Remember, this is your opportunity to turn a dissatisfied customer into a loyal and satisfied customer.

✧ Give the customer a chance to share their concerns, frustrations and feelings.

2. Empathize & Apologize

✧ For example, a retail sales clerk can say something like, *"I understand how frustrating it can be when you drive all the way across town to buy that laptop and you get here and we are sold out of that model."*

✧ Acknowledge the customer's concerns or problem. *"I am really sorry that you had this experience. I can see how this could be very frustrating for you."*

✧ A simple "I'm sorry" can go a long way toward reducing the customer's anger and frustration. **Until a customer hears those words, he or she may not be ready to move toward resolving the problem.**

✧ If you are dealing with the situation in person, nod your head to demonstrate that you are hearing what they are saying.

✧ Express sincere concern. You understand the impact on the customer and their business/department.

3. Don't Make Excuses

✧ The customer wants a solution, NOT an excuse or someone to blame.

✧ The customer isn't concerned with your problems.

✧ It looks bad for your organization, no matter which area or areas are at fault!

✧ **YOU** are the company to the customer.

4. Ask Questions

✧ For example, "*What specifically happened when the system went down? We want to make sure we solve the right problem.*"

✧ You want to respond quickly, but you also want to make sure you understand the problem in order to offer the appropriate solution.

✧ You may need to understand specific information.

✧ Confirm that you have an accurate understanding of the "real" problem.

✧ By asking questions and sincerely listening, you have involved the customer in solving the problem.

5. Agree to a Course of Action

✧ For example, "*We can do a couple of things to get you back on track and correct the problem. Do these work for you?*"

✧ Provide some possible solutions to address the concerns. Confirm that the solutions will meet your customer's needs and expectations.

✧ If you are not sure how to resolve the issue, do not be afraid to ask others for help, even if the original problem was your fault.

✧ Make sure that when you commit to an action/solution that you involve the proper people/departments, especially if you are counting on their support or action to follow through to satisfy the customer.

6. Check to Make Sure Action Is Completed

✧ It is not always possible to follow up on every customer interaction, but an occasional call to a customer who had a problem will go a long way in establishing a reputation as an organization that truly cares for its customers.

✧ You could select a small sample of customers, make calls and say, *"I just wanted to make sure that the actions we took met your needs. Is there anything else we can do to help?"*

✧ The objective is to find out if the customer was completely satisfied with the action taken to resolve the problem.

Even after there has been a problem, a customer is very likely to return to the business if the problem was resolved to their satisfaction in a timely manner.

Even after there has been a problem, a customer is very likely to return to the business if the problem was resolved to their satisfaction in a timely manner.

Recently, I heard of a story that surfaced in a small Texas town around Christmas time. For many years, a cranky old man frequented a local Luby's™ restaurant. All of the waitresses, except for one, would refuse to wait on this customer. He was impossible to please and often upset other waitresses. This one Luby's waitress found a way to not just endure the customer, but to truly serve and care for him. She was able to see beyond the surface and showed some concern, even though it was never returned by the old man.

Several weeks went by and the old man failed to show up for his regular meal at Luby's. She later learned that he had passed away and left quite a surprise. This old man had left the waitress $50,000 and a nice car in his will. When asked about this gift, the waitress just stated that she learned to deal with the old man and simply smiled and took care of his requests.

Remember, when you encounter an unhappy customer, apply the six steps discussed in this chapter. Your chances of turning the situation around and ending up with a customer who is a fan of your organization will go up significantly!

Be Part of a Winning Team

Everyone wants to be part of a winning team. From our early years, we learn that it is much more fun to win than lose when competing on a sports team. Some of the same things that make up a winning sports team can contribute to having a successful team at work.

Share the Burden

Picture your favorite basketball team playing in the NCAA Basketball Finals. On the court, there will be individuals who are great on defense and can prevent the best from reaching the basket. Others will be outstanding on the offensive end, knocking down three-point shots or dunking over the top of the opponent. Do you think the team would win if the defensive stars decided they would just wait under the other team's net for the action to come to them? No. That would leave other members of the team short-handed trying to score.

For some reason, some people think the same way in the workplace. They have their favorite jobs or tasks and do everything to avoid the things they don't like. The best teams win only after every member jumps in to help accomplish the overall goals.

I also have seen basketball teams fail when one "superstar" thinks he or she must be the one to take every shot. Eventually, the other team figures this out and double- or triple-teams them, knowing they are not likely to pass to a teammate. The same thing happens at the office. You may have a co-worker who thinks he or she is the only one who can do a particular job correctly. This can also be a leader who has never learned to delegate to the members of his or her team.

The key to success on any team is to spread the work around, trying to take advantage of each person's strengths while developing their weaknesses.

If you want to make yourself a valuable member of your team, take time to learn about your co-workers' jobs so you are ready to jump in and help out when the need arises.

The key to success on any team is to spread the work around, trying to take advantage of each person's strengths while developing their weaknesses. Learn to share the burden.

Celebrate the Victories

There is nothing quite like a win to get everyone excited and focused on the mission. It does not matter if the team is undefeated or trying to get their first win of the season. A "W" in the win/loss column is a great motivator!

Many of you have probably been in the room when a sibling or another child was learning to take their first steps. They hold on to the edge of the coffee table while attempting to gain their balance. Then it happens! They let go of the table and take two or three steps on their own. What happens in the room? Everyone goes crazy! Applause and cheers for the child's first steps.

What would you think if the mother or father looked at the child and said, "Let me know when you reach the other side of the room" and then went back to reading the paper?

Unfortunately, that is how many organizations handle small victories that occur on their teams every day. There is such a focus on the larger end goals that we fail to celebrate the wins that help us move in that direction. When you hear or see one of your co-workers doing a great job that results in a satisfied customer, celebrate and let others know about this success.

This is especially true if you work in a department that partners with other groups. When you hear a story of a satisfied customer, go out of your way to pass that praise on to co-workers in the other department. This is a great way to build on your relationship. The other group will be more willing to go the extra mile when you need their future help if they think that you are truly partners.

Stop the Finger Pointing

What do most people do when they are confronted with a problem or customer complaint? The most common reaction is to immediately look for someone else to blame. This is a basic human behavior that is mastered by the time we learn to speak. I can still remember my younger brother trying to get me in trouble with my parents by attempting to pass the blame for something he had clearly done.

When you are discussing a problem with a customer, they really don't care who is at fault. They just want a solution. When a customer brings a problem to your attention, the correct response is to apologize on behalf of the entire organization or company. Avoid the temptation to say, "I'm sorry that Jimmy over in accounting messed up your invoice." Instead, the correct response would be, "I am sorry that we made a mistake on your invoice. I will work with our accounting team to correct this right away."

Cut Each Other Some Slack!

One of the challenges of working on a team is that we are interacting with humans who are never perfect. If you are doing anything challenging or worthwhile, mistakes are going to happen. There are a lot of things that influence the behavior we hear and see in our co-workers.

You may have a team member who is very easy to work with most of the time. One day this co-worker comes into the office and gives you a hard time for something you knew nothing about. Your first reaction would be to defend yourself and give him or her a piece of your mind.

That is when you need to take a deep breath and let them return to their work area. You are only seeing through a small window of what is going on in their life. For all you know, they could have just found out that a loved one was diagnosed with a serious life-threatening disease. If someone is acting out of character and doing things you normally do not see them doing, give them a break. Wait to see if they come to their senses.

That does not excuse co-workers who are routinely abusive or act in inappropriate ways. I would guess that you are faced with situations of this kind very infrequently. If left alone, most people will realize they were out of line and will eventually apologize.

Get the Big Picture!

There is an exercise we use when we conduct team-building retreats. During this "Helium Pole" event, the participants are asked to line up on either side of a long, light pole such as those that are used to put up a tent. They are asked to extend their hands and place a finger from each hand under the pole to support it. The object is for the team to lower the pole to the ground.

Seems simple, doesn't it? Some groups will take 30 minutes or more to accomplish the goal. I won't go into the details, but one of the key secrets to success happens when each team member on the pole begins to focus on the entire effort instead of just the 12 inches of pole that is located in front of them. The application in the workplace is that we are more successful reaching our goals when we learn to see the big picture and attempt to understand what other members of the team are doing.

One of the other natural reactions during this exercise is for members on one end of the pole to start blaming the opposite end when the pole begins to rise. I am not aware of any individual attempting to sabotage this event, but problems do occur whenever you attempt to get more than a couple of people working together to accomplish a goal. Assume that your co-workers, even those in another department, are honestly trying to do their best to perform their jobs and help the team reach the overall goal.

Working on a team can be fun and frustrating at the same time. Strive to be a positive, patient member of each team you have the privilege of joining. You want to build a reputation of being a great team player. Remember in grade school how you didn't want to be the last one picked for a game of kickball?

Focus on the
Inner Circles

Every person, regardless of their title or position within the organization, has one thing in common with the rest of the team: We can all place our different relationships and work tasks into the three circles as shown below.

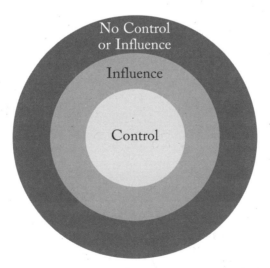

No Control
or Influence

Influence

Control

The inner circle represents the parts of our life that we control. The next circle contains those things that we do not control, but we can influence. The outer circle represents the things we neither control nor influence.

It is amazing how many people spend most of their time focused on that outer circle even though there is a limited amount of time each day. Things out of your control could include your company's future location, the list of projects and services that will be provided next year, or who will be appointed to lead your department. We may have some influence if someone asks our opinion, but generally, those decisions will be made regardless of whether we agree with them or not.

> *Doesn't it make more sense to focus our time and talents on the things we can control ... or at least influence?*

Doesn't it make more sense to focus our time and talents on the things we can control ... or at least influence? There are a few things that everyone has in their inner circle. Let's explore several of those areas. For example:

1. Your employer is a major electronics retailer and you work on the floor interacting with customers every day. A customer comes up to you and asks for a particular item that is an accessory to a popular MP3 player. You check the shelf, but you are out of that item. You have noticed that this has happened several times in the past month for this same product. Which circle does this fall into?

The answer is both the inner "control" and the middle "influence" circles. You "control" your response to the customer. This could include checking other locations, offering a rain check, or finding out when you expect more stock to arrive.

You may have some influence over the ordering process. Instead of just forgetting about this problem once the customer leaves, you could speak to the department leader and find out if it would be possible to increase the regular order quantity of this item so you won't run out again.

2. You work in a call center providing support for a wide variety of products. You notice that you are receiving an unusually high number of calls regarding the setup and installation of a new product. What do you do?

You have two options:

   a. Continue taking the calls and solving the customer problems as they come up. You may even think, "I work in the call center. It's not my job to improve the product or instructions."

   b. Take the initiative. Track down the documentation that is shipped with that particular product. Write a short note with your suggestions on how to improve the instructions, which then will cut down on the number of phone calls coming into your call center. Be sure to include the data about the frequency of calls dealing with this topic. Send the note to your team leader if that is the appropriate path for communication. If it is acceptable to interact directly with other departments, send the note to the leader of the group who handles product documentation.

I would hope you would choose option "b." Most leaders are always on the lookout for a front-line employee who is interested in improving the company and not just collecting a paycheck.

Leaders also become frustrated with team members who are constantly bringing problems to their attention. You may even be labeled as a "whiner" or "complainer." How do you avoid this? Whenever you feel the desire to bring a problem to your leadership's attention, make sure you include your recommended solution to resolve the situation.

> *Whenever you feel the desire to bring a problem to your leadership's attention, make sure you include your recommended solution to resolve the situation.*

3. You work for a doctor's office at the front desk checking in patients and preparing charts. The current privacy regulations are forcing you to jump through hoops every time you have to create a new patient in your computer system.

Although you could provide your feedback, this is probably an area that falls in the third circle: Something you neither control nor influence. Why should you waste your energy and possibly annoy your co-workers by constantly complaining about this process? Let it go and focus on things you can control or influence.

Focus your attention on the inner two circles, leaving the outer circles for people who have the chance to change or influence these areas.

Provide Your Input

Not all organizations have a method of asking for ideas or suggestions from all members of the team, but if you work for a company that does, take advantage of this opportunity and provide your feedback. This could be in the form of a suggestion box, an employee satisfaction survey, or informal discussions with your leadership. Be ready to present your ideas in an organized way, but don't get upset if you don't see things implemented within your timeframe. It takes organizations time to evaluate suggestions and employee feedback, then to figure out how some changes fit in with the company's overall direction and objectives.

Focus your attention on the inner two circles, leaving the outer circles for people who have the chance to change or influence these areas.

Get Organized!

One of the most significant factors that a leader considers when writing performance reviews or considering someone for a raise or promotion is, "Do they get things done as assigned or promised?"

We all have a lot going on, especially if you are working on the front line interfacing with customers most of the day. There are always multiple things competing for your time:

1. You are working with a customer and there are five more waiting in line.

2. Your boss just asked you to update her on a customer issue that you handled earlier in the week.

3. You are part of a work team that has been asked to come up with a way of reducing the number of customer complaints.

4. The HR department has sent you a third reminder that you must complete a new mandatory safety-training class online.

If you are like me, there are times you wish you could clone yourself and send the clone out to finish half of your tasks. Unfortunately, that is not possible, at least with today's technology. We all have 525,600 minutes in a year. (Unless it is a Leap Year when we get a bonus 1,440 minutes.) The average reader will consume 120 of those minutes reading this book. You will sleep for at least 153,300 minutes this year and spend 21,900 minutes in traffic if you are fortunate to live within 30 minutes of your job. What is the point?

The older you get, the more you will realize that life moves at a very fast pace. I can remember like it was yesterday when my two kids were born. Now my son, Tony, will be in high school next year and daughter, Holly, will be in the 6th grade.

One of the keys to making the most of the minutes we all have is to get organized.

One of the keys to making the most of the minutes we all have is to get organized. These basic principles will help make the most of your day:

✦ **Be Here Now!** Most people spend a large percentage of their day thinking about what's next or where they will be the next day or week. I learned this lesson in a painful way while I was in college. My freshman year I was crazy enough to schedule a Monday morning calculus class. I had taken calculus in high school, so I thought it would be easy. I slipped into the habit of skipping that class on occasion. It took me most of the semester to realize that this was not a good use of my time. I soon figured out that for every 50-minute lecture I missed, it took at least three hours of my time to find the notes from a classmate, read the chapter, teach myself the materials, and study everything because I was not sure what the professor was going to put on the test.

I always encourage people to do everything possible to focus on the task that needs to be completed. If you are at work, try to give it everything you have. If you are in school, pay attention to your teacher or professor and make the most of every class period.

✦ **Maintain a To-Do List.** If you are looking for something simple to do that will pay back a great return, I recommend developing the discipline of keeping a to-do list. I have to admit that I don't always keep my list updated, but anytime there are more than a handful of tasks on my plate, I return to the habit of writing down the tasks. Do you ever lie in bed at night and have a hard time falling asleep because you keep thinking of things you need to do the next day?

The to-do list that I use is very straightforward and has the following columns:

 ✧ **Status.** I use this column to mark "Done" next to the tasks that have been completed. I keep things on my list for a week or so after they are done and then delete them from the list. This gives me a sense of accomplishment and takes care of any question as to whether or not I have completed a particular task.

 ✧ **Area or project.** These can be things around the house (Area = home) or particular projects or clients that I am involved with.

❖ **Due Date.** When do I have to have this item completed?

❖ **Description.** A short description of the task or project. (5-10 words)

❖ **Priority.** I define the priority this way:

  ♦ A = Critical. Must be done. No option.

  ♦ B = Important. Date may be adjusted to make room for the critical items.

  ♦ C = Smaller tasks that I don't want to forget, but they are not critical. Often I will group a lot of the smaller tasks together and knock them off all at once.

What do you gain by maintaining a to-do list?

❖ Reduce the chance that something will drop through the cracks or be forgotten.

❖ Reduce stress by writing things down so that you can focus all your energy on one task at a time.

❖ Prioritize your tasks to ensure you get the most important tasks completed on schedule.

✦ **Set Goals.** What is the difference between someone who is always an average employee and one who is moving forward and going places in life? One key difference is that the employee who is successful usually takes some time to set goals in life. There is a simple process I use in my time-management workshops to help people set goals in various areas of their lives.

Step 1: List the different roles you play. Most of us have 4-5 roles that we fulfill on a daily or monthly basis. This could include things like:

- ✧ Spouse
- ✧ Parent
- ✧ Son or daughter
- ✧ Friend
- ✧ Volunteer in a church or civic organization
- ✧ Employee
- ✧ Team leader

Step 2: Define a goal for each role. Many of you may have spent time coming up with goals at work or for your career, but very few of us ever set goals for other areas of our life. In our class, everyone writes down one goal for each of the roles they play, committing to complete them within the next 30-60 days.

Step 3: Monitor your progress. At least once a week, pull out your goal sheet and see how you are doing. If it would help, share your goals with a friend or co-worker and ask them to hold you accountable to reaching your goals.

I have found that spending a few minutes setting goals in each area of your life will help you maintain balance between work and your personal life. An individual who has a stable, balanced life is going to be a better employee.

What is the connection between being organized and delivering great customer service? It is difficult to be a productive team member serving customers if you don't have your personal act together. Stress due to too many things wanting your time can be a distraction and take away from a positive, customer-friendly attitude.

Pick Your
Battles Wisely

If there is one lesson that I have learned since entering the workplace, it's realizing that not everything is worth a fight. I wish they could figure out how to teach this in school, but they probably never will. Success in life is not always about being right! Let me share a personal experience to illustrate this point.

Several years ago while I was working at Walt Disney World, I was put in charge of a team to develop the contingency plan for the Y2K event. For those of you who don't remember this, it was probably the biggest "non-event" in my lifetime. There were a lot of people predicting the end of life as we knew it when the clock struck midnight on Dec. 31, 1999. There were rumors that power would fail, computer software would stop working, and there would be mass panic across the globe. With the exception of some minor hiccups,

Success in life is not always about being right!

Jan. 1, 2000, came and went without a major problem. We will never know if it would have been worse had we not done so much preparation for that day.

My team of five "Cast Members" (the Disney term for employee) had the job of developing an organized process to help everyone at Disney World handle a wide variety of potential situations. We were the "What If" team and went around to each area and asked questions such as, "What happens if the monorail is halfway between Epcot and Magic Kingdom when we lose power?" or "How should the hundreds of retail stores respond if the main cash register system stops working?" or "How will hundreds of Disney buses refuel if there is no power to run the gas pumps?"

We spent several months developing a well-thought-out process to uncover the biggest threats, creating manual work-arounds to continue operations until life returned to normal. My team was very proud of its process and felt we had thought about every possible angle.

That was when the problem occurred. My boss asked to meet with the team to review the contingency planning process and tools. We spent an hour presenting our hard work to him, expecting nothing less than, "Wow. This is great. I can't think of anything I would change!"

I was not prepared for what happened next. We were so sure we had thought of everything that when my boss suggested a slight change in our approach, it caught me off guard. It was only a minor adjustment to one of our planning worksheets, but I was convinced that our variation was the right answer. This is when I wish someone had taught me the value of strategically picking your battles!

We had some discussions about this suggestion and then we concluded the team meeting. I decided I was going to show my boss who was right and I began to argue about this point, which escalated into a heated discussion. Needless to say, this exchange of words harmed my relationship with my boss. We ultimately recovered from this and made things right, but the damage had been done.

Looking back on that day, I can see some things that I wish I had done differently.

✦ **Let it go!** The minor change that my boss suggested would have been insignificant in the overall big picture. Even if my way had been the better solution, his way would have worked just as well. So many of us get caught up in proving a point that we forget to look at the long-term impact of our actions.

✦ **Watch my words.** I really like this quote by Lady Dorothy Nevill: "The real art of conversation is not only to say the right thing in the right place, but to leave unsaid the wrong thing at the tempting moment." How many times have you said something and then immediately wished you could have taken the words back? Unfortunately, I have stuck my foot in my mouth on many occasions! To keep this from happening again, think before

> *"The real art of conversation is not only to say the right thing in the right place, but to leave unsaid the wrong thing at the tempting moment."*
>
> – Lady Dorothy Nevill

you speak or e-mail. Ask yourself, "Who will benefit and who will be harmed by my words?"

✦ **Look beyond the moment.** When you are tempted to go to battle with someone over an issue, ask yourself: "Will this really matter 5, 10 or 20 years from now?" So many times we think the current issue is so important when, in reality, no one will remember the outcome days or years from now. Take the long-term view of your work and how you respond to challenges.

There is one exception to what I have been sharing. If the area in question involves your morals, values or ethics, then it may be an appropriate battle to fight. The truth is that most of our arguments do not fall into this category, but are simply a matter of pride.

You may be asking: "So what does this have to do with customer service?" Just as in your relationships with your boss, co-workers, family or friends, the same principles apply when you interact with customers.

There may be times when you know for a fact that you are correct when dealing with a customer, but you must still remember to consider the long-term value of that customer. On occasion, we may have to give up a small sale or offer a replacement product with the larger goal of keeping the customer for a lifetime of potential business.

People often ask me, "Is the customer always right?" My response is, "No, but they are always the customer, and they are the reason companies exist and why each of us has a job."

Wrapping It Up

I hope you have found a couple of nuggets of truth in this book that will help you become more effective, both personally and professionally. The success of your organization depends on you and the way you handle every interaction with a customer, vendor, team member, or potential customer. Remember these ideas:

1. **Be a difference maker.** Anyone can use their job and their daily tasks to make a positive difference in the lives of those they come in contact with.

2. **Serve each other.** Although it is rare and sometimes difficult, learn to serve your fellow team members and customers. Put other's needs ahead of your own and trust that those who do the right thing will win in the end.

3. **Leave it at the door.** We all have our challenges and personal issues. Learn to check that bag at the door and give your employer and teammates all of your energy.

4. **Show some urgency.** Remember that the No. 1 customer turnoff is a long wait. We are dealing with impatient people who want what you are selling, and they want it now.

5. **Engage the customer.** Go out of your way to talk to and interact with your customers.

6. **Be kind.** (Remember your grandma!) Actively look for opportunities to show that you care for others.

7. **Turn difficult customers around.** Every time you have the opportunity to deal with a difficult or angry customer, take it as a challenge to turn them around. Remember to use your listening skills!

8. **Build your team.** Use the team concept of service, then work together to provide the best possible service to your customers.

9. **Focus on the inner circles.** Apply your talents and energy toward things that you can either control or influence. Leave the rest to someone else.

10. **Get organized.** Develop your own practices to help you make the most of every day.

11. **Pick your battles wisely.** Remember, success in life and work is not always about being "right."

Have fun delivering
Service Where It Counts!

Customer Centered Consulting Group, Inc., helps companies of all sizes develop exceptional customer service, effective leadership, and simple processes to enhance

Customer Centered
Consulting Group, Inc.

profitability. Headquartered in Frisco, Texas, and formed in 1999, the Group's outstanding track record in customer service, human resources and business operations distinguishes it from the competition by providing a wide variety of services, including:

✦ **Team-Building Retreats** – Getting any group of individuals to work together toward a common goal is difficult, but spending time together working through challenging exercises will help. During this half- or full-day session, we work to improve communication, understanding and overall team effectiveness while having fun.

✦ **Customer-Service Training** – Provide half-day and full-day interactive training sessions to re-focus the attention on the customer while reinforcing policies and procedures that deal with the treatment of your customers.

✦ **Customer Surveys** – Design and conduct a customer survey to find out how your customers really feel about your organization and help identify opportunities for improvement.

✦ **Employee Satisfaction Surveys** – Design and conduct an employee survey, gaining high participation rates and honest feedback because of the neutral, outside facilitation of the entire process. Detailed results and a proven action-planning process help make the survey a key part of any organization's annual planning process.

✦ **Keynote Addresses** – Address your convention, conference or internal meetings about increasing customer service and building market leadership.

To learn how Customer Centered Consulting Group can make a difference in your bottom line, please visit the web site, call, or send an e-mail to info@cccginc.com.

Customer Centered Consulting Group, Inc.
5729 Lebanon Dr., Suite 144 PMB 222
Frisco, TX 75034
(469) 633-9833 – voice   (469) 633-9843 – fax
www.cccginc.com

About the Author

David Reed brings a unique combination of an engineering education, real-world experience, and entertaining presentation skills to each client engagement. Chemical Engineering and Computer Science degrees from Texas A&M University provide the technical, process-minded approach to reviewing work processes.

Over 15 years ago, David realized he wanted to ultimately start a company that focused on two areas: 1) Customer Service and 2) Leadership. He believes that if any organization can do a good job in these areas, they will ultimately be successful.

David served with Andersen Consulting and Exxon, and in senior leadership roles with several smaller companies. His last stop prior to starting his own business was with Walt Disney World in Orlando.

Since starting Customer Centered Consulting Group, Inc. in 1999, David has provided business consulting, training and speaking services for a wide variety of companies, including:

- ✦ State Farm Insurance
- ✦ Concentra
- ✦ General Motors
- ✦ Crosstex Energy
- ✦ City of Missouri City
- ✦ Prestonwood Christian Academy
- ✦ Valencia Community College Foundation

- ✦ Sky Ranch Camps
- ✦ Halliburton
- ✦ Texas National Guard
- ✦ Devereux Foundation
- ✦ Eckerd Youth Alternatives
- ✦ Toshiba
- ✦ Florida's Department of Children & Families

David is the author of three additional easy-read, customer-service books: *Monday Morning Customer Service, Business Meets the Bible: Customer Service,* and *A Culture of Service.* He resides in Frisco, Texas, with his wife and two children and travels throughout the country conducting customer-service training and providing consulting services.

Accelerate Inspired Sales & Service Resources:

Monday Morning Customer Service takes you on a journey of eight lessons that demonstrate how to take care of customers so they keep coming back. **$14.95**

A Culture of Service shows you how to create an atmosphere where customers will be loyal to your organization. **$14.95**

Listen Up, Customer Service is a step-by-step guide to improving customer relations while, at the same time, increasing employee satisfaction. **$9.95**

You Gotta Get in the Game … Playing to Win in Business, Sales and Life provides direction on how to get into and win the game of life and business. **$14.95**

Influential Selling – How to Win in Today's Selling Environment is designed to stimulate new ways of thinking about your selling efforts and positioning them to align with your client. It will provide your team with new strategies and activities that will help you start winning today. **$14.95**

180 Ways to Walk the Customer Service Talk is packed with proven strategies and tips. This powerful handbook will get everyone "walking the customer service talk." **$9.95**

Orchestrating Attitude: Getting the Best from Yourself and Others translates the abstract into the actionable. It cuts through the clutter to deliver inspiration and application so you can orchestrate your attitude … and your success. **$9.95**

Goal Setting for Results addresses the fundamentals of setting and achieving your goal of moving yourself and your organization from where you are to where you want (and need) to be! **$9.95**

The CornerStone Perpetual Calendar, a compelling collection of quotes about leadership and life, is perfect for office desks, school and home countertops. Offering a daily dose of inspiration, this terrific calendar makes the perfect gift or motivational reward. **$14.95**

The CornerStone Leadership Collection of Cards is designed to make it easy for you to show appreciation for your team, clients and friends. The awesome photography and your personal message written inside will create a lasting impact. Pack/19 (19 styles/1 each) **$29.95**
Posters also available.

Visit www.**CornerStoneLeadership**.com for
additional books and resources.